Blackbeard

and the
Pirates of the Caribbean

John Malam

QEB Publishing

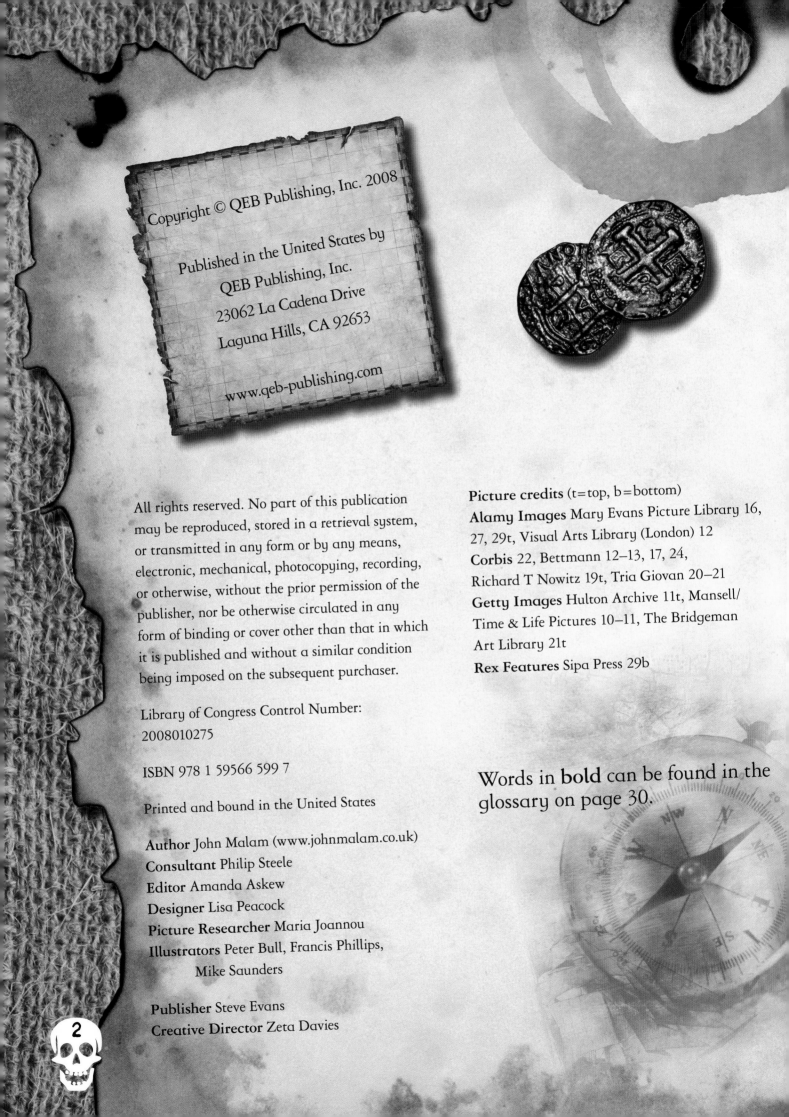

Copyright © QEB Publishing, Inc. 2008

Published in the United States by
QEB Publishing, Inc.
23062 La Cadena Drive
Laguna Hills, CA 92653

www.qeb-publishing.com

Library of Congress Control Number:
2008010275

ISBN 978 1 59566 599 7

Printed and bound in the United States

Author John Malam (www.johnmalam.co.uk)
Consultant Philip Steele
Editor Amanda Askew
Designer Lisa Peacock
Picture Researcher Maria Joannou
Illustrators Peter Bull, Francis Phillips,
　　　　　Mike Saunders

Publisher Steve Evans
Creative Director Zeta Davies

Picture credits (t=top, b=bottom)
Alamy Images Mary Evans Picture Library 16, 27, 29t, Visual Arts Library (London) 12
Corbis 22, Bettmann 12–13, 17, 24, Richard T Nowitz 19t, Tria Giovan 20–21
Getty Images Hulton Archive 11t, Mansell/Time & Life Pictures 10–11, The Bridgeman Art Library 21t
Rex Features Sipa Press 29b

Words in **bold** can be found in the glossary on page 30.

CONTENTS

PIRATE ATTACK! 4

PIRATES OF THE CARIBBEAN: 1690-1730 6

PIRATE SHIP: A DEN OF THIEVES 8

SIR HENRY MORGAN: THE KING'S FAVOURITE 10

EDWARD TEACH: THE MOST NOTORIOUS PIRATE 12

LIFE ON BOARD SHIP 14

PIRATE HAVENS 16

SAMUEL BELLAMY: THE PIRATE PRINCE 18

PIRATE PRIZES: SHIPS AND THEIR CARGOES 20

JOHN RACKHAM: THE PIRATE IN FANCY CLOTHES 22

ANNE BONNY AND MARY READ 24

PUNISHMENTS FOR PRISONERS AND PIRATES 26

PIRATE HUNTERS: THE END OF PIRATES
   IN THE CARIBBEAN 28

GLOSSARY 30

INDEX 32

Pirate attack!

In November 1717, a pirate ship sailed off the coast of Martinique Island, in the Caribbean Sea.

Its captain was Edward Teach, known as Blackbeard. His ship was a **sloop**—a small, fast, **vessel** with a single **mast**, 12 **cannon**, and a **crew** of about 120 pirates.

A larger ship came into view, and Blackbeard set a course toward it. It was the *Concorde*, a French **merchant ship**. It was packed with more than 400 slaves from Africa. The *Concorde* was well armed, but after four months crossing the Atlantic Ocean, the crew was in no mood for a fight. Blackbeard fired his cannon as a warning, and the captain of the *Concorde* surrendered his ship without a struggle.

⬆ The Concorde *was bigger and better armed than Blackbeard's sloop—but Blackbeard was determined to seize it.*

4

The *Concorde* was carrying treasure—about 19 pounds of gold dust, plus silver and jewellery. The ship's cabin boy, 15-year-old Louis Arot, told Blackbeard where it was hidden. Instead of sailing away with the rest of the *Concorde*'s crew, Arot became one of Blackbeard's pirates.

The pirates put the *Concorde*'s crew and slaves onto Blackbeard's sloop, and let them sail away. The *Concorde* was the **prize**, and it became Blackbeard's **flagship**. It came with about 16 cannon, but Blackbeard increased the number to 40, and he gave the ship a new name —the *Queen Anne's Revenge*.

Pirates of the Caribbean: 1690–1730

Blackbeard was one of many pirates who terrorized the Caribbean.

For about 40 years, from 1690 to 1730, sea-robbers raided towns and **plundered** ships that crossed their path. This was the Golden Age of Caribbean piracy.

Before the Caribbean became the haunt of pirates, it was home to **buccaneers**. They were mainly English, French, and Dutch men who lived on the Caribbean's many islands. In the 1600s, some island **governors** gave the buccaneers permission to raid Spanish ships, which they did with great success. When buccaneers began plundering ships from *every* country, the governors tried to put an end to their activities—without success.

North America

Caribbean Islands

Caribbean Sea

South America

⬆ *Caribbean pirates cruised the waters around the sea's many islands, from the northeast coast of South America to the east coast of the United States.*

Some buccaneers carried on raiding without permission—and that is when they became pirates. Hundreds of men and a few women sailed as pirates in the Caribbean. Like Blackbeard, they were attracted by thoughts of rich pickings. For a few years, they were masters of the Caribbean.

ROGUES' GALLERY

Henry Morgan
Active as a buccaneer
1665–1671

Samuel Bellamy
Active as a pirate
1715–1717

Edward Teach
Active as a pirate
1716–1718

John Rackham
Active as a pirate
1718–1720

Anne Bonny
Active as a pirate
1719–1720

Mary Read
Active as a pirate
1719–1720

Pirate ship: a den of thieves

Most pirate ships in the Caribbean were sloops. Pirates used sloops because they were faster than the merchant ships they raided.

Once a pirate sloop set course toward a merchant ship, it soon caught up with the bigger, slower vessel, as Blackbeard did when he attacked the *Concorde*. A fast ship also meant that pirates could escape to safety when navy warships came after them.

➤ *A typical 12-gun sloop used by Caribbean pirates. It was about 60 feet in length and weighed about 100 tons.*

Windlass

The best sloops were built in the shipyards of Jamaica and Bermuda. They had single masts and could sail in shallow water. They could come close to land without getting stuck, and hide in sheltered bays. Pirate captains fitted their sloops with many cannon, which they took from captured ships.

Anchor

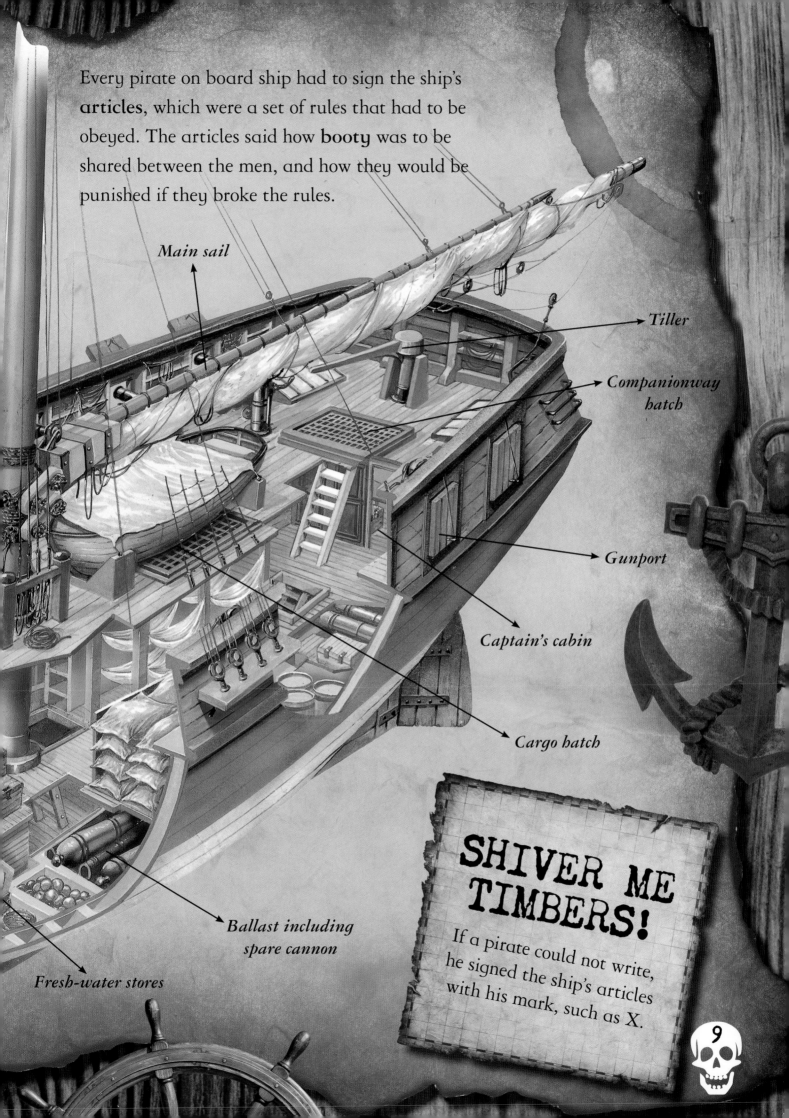

Every pirate on board ship had to sign the ship's **articles**, which were a set of rules that had to be obeyed. The articles said how **booty** was to be shared between the men, and how they would be punished if they broke the rules.

Main sail

Tiller

Companionway hatch

Gunport

Captain's cabin

Cargo hatch

Ballast including spare cannon

Fresh-water stores

SHIVER ME TIMBERS!

If a pirate could not write, he signed the ship's articles with his mark, such as X.

9

Sir Henry Morgan: the king's favourite

Henry Morgan was a buccaneer. At the end of 1667, the governor of Jamaica, Thomas Modyford, gave him permission to attack Spanish ships, since he believed Spain was planning to invade the island.

Morgan had other plans. In January 1668, he raided a Spanish town on Cuba and then, with a force of 500 men, captured Portobello, a Spanish port on the coast of Panama. He returned to Jamaica with a fortune said to be worth $200,000.

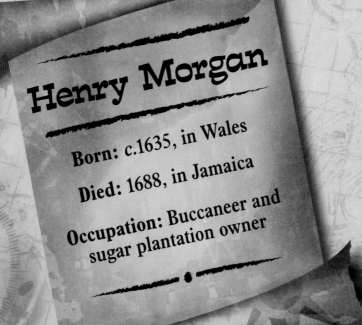

Henry Morgan

Born: c.1635, in Wales

Died: 1688, in Jamaica

Occupation: Buccaneer and sugar plantation owner

↑ In 1669, Morgan attacked and burned Spanish ships off the coast of Venezuela, and took 20,000 silver pesos *from them.*

In 1670, Governor Modyford sent Morgan back to Panama, this time with 2,000 men. Unfortunately for Morgan, the Spaniards had moved their treasure out of the city, leaving little to steal. Worse was to come—Spain and England had signed a **peace treaty**. When Morgan returned to Jamaica, he was arrested and sent to England.

⬆ *Morgan forced the citizens of Portobello to hand over 100,000 silver pesos. Only after the ransom had been paid, did Morgan leave their town.*

Morgan spent two years in the Tower of London, England, but was never charged with any crime. In fact, he became a hero for his actions against Spain, England's old enemy. On his release, Morgan was **knighted** by King Charles II, and in 1675, he returned to Jamaica as the island's lieutenant-governor.

11

Edward Teach: the most notorious pirate

Edward Teach, better known as Blackbeard, was a tall man with wild eyes.

His long, black beard was twisted with ribbons, lengths of smoking **fuse** poked out from under his hat, and across his chest were slings that held six pistols. Blackbeard looked tough, and he was tough.

⬆ *A flintlock pistol fired a small ball of solid lead, and took a long time to reload. In close combat, the handle was used as a club.*

Blackbeard's reign of terror began in 1716, when he joined the pirate Benjamin Hornigold. Blackbeard was soon in command of a sloop, which he replaced with a larger ship, the *Queen Anne's Revenge*. As Blackbeard plundered ships and towns along the east coast of North America, he earned a reputation as a fierce pirate. He was so ruthless that he even **marooned** his own men, and made off with all the booty.

Blackbeard met his end in November 1718, when he was tracked down by Lieutenant Robert Maynard of the British Royal Navy. He was killed by a sword blow from one of Maynard's men, and his head was cut off and put on the **bow** of Maynard's ship for all to see.

Edward Teach
known as "Blackbeard"

Born: c.1680, in England

Died: 1718, off the coast of North Carolina, North America

Occupation: Pirate

◀ *Blackbeard's last moments, as he fights to the death with Lieutenant Maynard on board the Royal Navy ship the Jane.*

SHIVER ME TIMBERS!

A shipwreck, believed to be the *Queen Anne's Revenge*, was found in 1996. Archeologists are studying the wreck to see if it really could be Blackbeard's famous ship.

13

Life on board ship

Pirate sloops sailed with a **company**, or crew, of about 80 men.

The crew was very well organized and discipline was important. As well as agreeing to keep the ship's articles, each pirate knew his place in the company. The captain was in charge, helped by the **quartermaster**, who was second-in-command.

⬆ *Wooden barrels stored the crew's food and other supplies. Each one was made from pieces of strong wood, held together with iron hoops.*

There was always boring, everyday work for the men to do. Swords were kept sharp, cannon were cleaned and made ready for use, torn sails were mended, meals were prepared, and lookouts kept watch for ships and land.

⬅ *Sails were made from coarse cloth called canvas. Rips had to be stitched up.*

What the men wanted most of all was a chance to raise the ship's flag, or **Jolly Roger**, which was a sign that they were pirates. Pirate captains had their own flags, showing skulls, bones, swords, and wounded hearts, usually on a black background. These designs signaled "death" to anyone who resisted.

SHIVER ME TIMBERS!

Live sea turtles were kept on board some pirate ships. They were a source of fresh meat for Caribbean pirates.

PIRATE FLAGS

↓ The name "Jolly Roger" might come from the French words jolie rouge meaning "pretty red," or from the English word "roger" meaning "devil."

Edward Teach, known as Blackbeard

Bartholomew Roberts

John Rackham

Stede Bonnet

Pirate havens

Dotted around the Caribbean were safe havens where pirates anchored their ships and came ashore.

The buccaneers used Port Royal, on the island of Jamaica, as their den. In its **taverns**, they gambled and drank away the proceeds of their raids until, in 1692, the town was destroyed by an earthquake.

⬆ *Port Royal was destroyed by an earthquake, and much of the town was swallowed by the sea.*

In the Golden Age of piracy — the time of Blackbeard, Samuel Bellamy, John Rackham, and others—the island of New Providence became the Caribbean's major pirate haven.

Speak like a pirate

Ahoy! Shouted to a ship or a person to attract attention.

Avast! A command, meaning to stop doing something.

Davy Jones' Locker The bottom of the sea—home of shipwrecks and drowned sailors.

Land ho! Shouted by the ship's lookout when land was sighted.

Lubber A clumsy person not used to life at sea.

Mate A fellow sailor. Also an officer on a merchant or navy ship.

Swabber The lowest type of sailor, only fit for swabbing (mopping) the decks.

Their sloops took shelter in the island's shallow harbor, where the bigger pirate-hunting warships of the British Royal Navy could not enter. The island provided pirates with food, water, and timber. Bribes were given to the island's governors, and in return, the pirates were left alone.

By 1717, about 500 pirates used New Providence as their base. However, when Governor Woodes Rogers came to the island the following year, he hanged eight of them and **pardoned** those who gave up piracy. Some, including Blackbeard, fled to new havens.

SHIVER ME TIMBERS!

After leaving New Providence, Blackbeard made Ocracoke Island his base, from where he raided towns along the east coast of North America.

Woodes Rogers was originally a privateer. He had permission from the English government to raid Spanish ships and settlements.

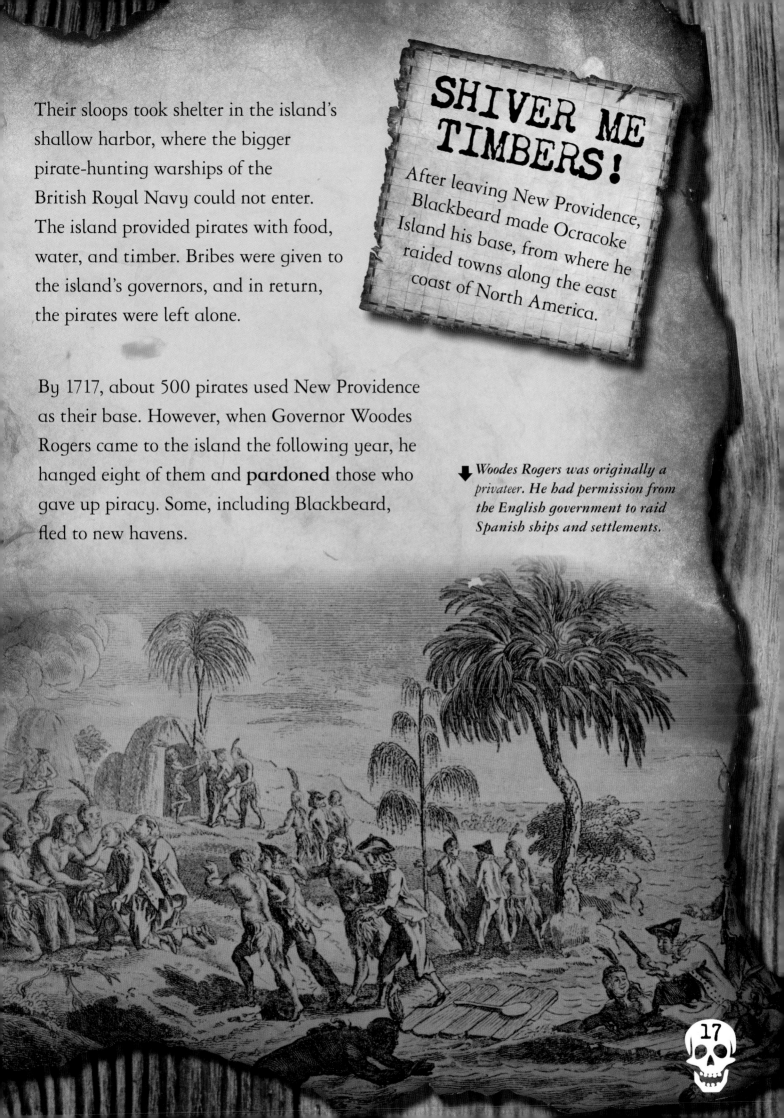

Samuel Bellamy:
the pirate prince

Samuel Bellamy was known as the prince of pirates by his men because he gave them equal shares in any loot he took.

In March 1717, Bellamy sailed from the pirate haven of New Providence in his sloop the *Sultana*. He was in search of a prize and it was not long before he spotted a large merchant ship. It was the *Whydah*, a slave ship. It had delivered its human cargo to Jamaica and was now bound for England, loaded with ivory, indigo, sugar, and thousands of Spanish gold and silver coins.

SHIVER ME TIMBERS!

The wreck of the *Whydah* was found by a treasure hunter in 1984. It was the first pirate ship found in the Caribbean, and some of its valuable treasure has been salvaged.

↑ The Whydah *ran aground, broke apart, and sank. Bellamy and 143 other pirates were drowned. Only two men survived.*

A Spanish gold coin and ring from the wreck of the Whydah. Thousands of coins, gold bars, and pieces of jewelry have been brought to the surface.

Samuel Bellamy

Born: 1689, in England

Died: 1717, off the coast of Massachusetts, North America

Occupation: Pirate

Bellamy chased the *Whydah* for three days, and captured it near the Bahamas. The ship was one of the most valuable prizes ever taken by a Caribbean pirate, and Bellamy made it his flagship. However, his luck soon ran out. In May 1717, the *Whydah* was wrecked in a storm. Bellamy and most of his crew were drowned, and the pirate treasure disappeared into Davy Jones' Locker—the bottom of the sea.

Pirate prizes: ships and their cargoes

On a clear day, a pirate lookout could see a ship up to 20 miles away.

It was important to identify the ship quickly. Pirate sloops kept well away from warships, which could be on anti-piracy patrol. What the pirates wanted was a merchant ship, and when one was sighted, they sailed toward it. As their sloop caught up with the prize, the pirates flew a false flag.

➤ *From high in the ship's rigging, a lookout kept watch for ships to raid as well as ships to avoid.*

This tricked the captain of the merchant ship into thinking that the sloop was friendly, so he did not try to escape. When the pirates were close, they raised their pirate flag and fired their cannon over the bow of the prize, hoping the captain would surrender without a fight.

➤ *Caribbean pirates fought with cutlass swords. They were slashing weapons and were sharp along one edge.*

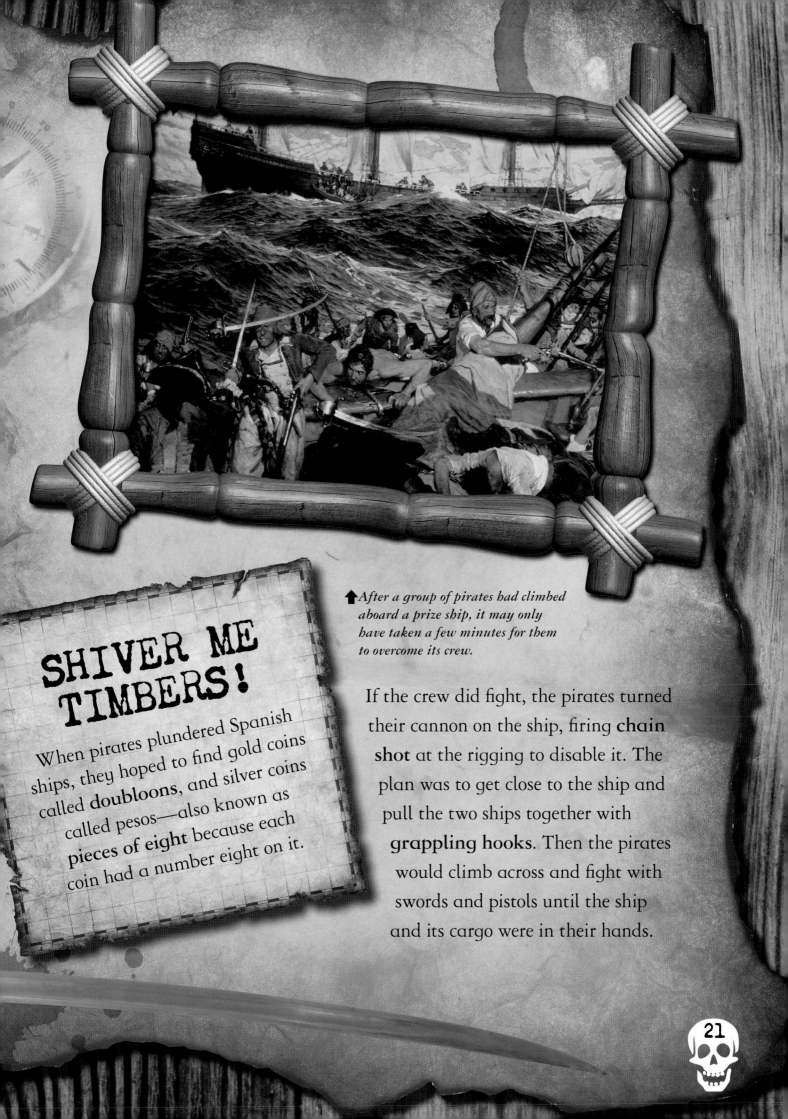

After a group of pirates had climbed aboard a prize ship, it may only have taken a few minutes for them to overcome its crew.

SHIVER ME TIMBERS!

When pirates plundered Spanish ships, they hoped to find gold coins called **doubloons**, and silver coins called pesos—also known as **pieces of eight** because each coin had a number eight on it.

If the crew did fight, the pirates turned their cannon on the ship, firing **chain shot** at the rigging to disable it. The plan was to get close to the ship and pull the two ships together with **grappling hooks**. Then the pirates would climb across and fight with swords and pistols until the ship and its cargo were in their hands.

John Rackham:
the pirate in fancy clothes

John, or Jack, Rackham wore striped shirts made from **calico**, which earned him the nickname "Calico Jack."

Rackham was one of the many pirates who used the island of New Providence as a base. When Woodes Rogers became the governor there in 1718, Rackham accepted his pardon and agreed to give up piracy. It did not last long. There was little work on the island, so Rackham went back to being a pirate.

⬆ *This early picture of John Rackham shows him as a tall, well-dressed man. He is carrying a sword and a pistol.*

John Rackham

Born: not known

Died: 1720, in Jamaica

Occupation: Pirate

John Rackham and his men were executed in 1720.

Rackham gathered a small crew, including women—Anne Bonny and Mary Read. They sailed on the sloop the *William*, and for a year they plundered small ships, but the booty did not amount to much.

A boarding axe used by pirates. It was also good for slicing through ropes.

Governor Rogers sent pirate hunter Captain Jonathan Barnet to catch Rackham. After a brief skirmish, Rackham and his crew were rounded up. Rackham and ten male pirates were hanged at Port Royal, Jamaica. His body was left hanging at the entrance to the harbor as a grim warning to others.

23

Anne Bonny and Mary Read

Anne Bonny and Mary Read were brought up as boys.

Bonny married a penniless sailor, and they made their way to the island of New Providence, where she met the pirate John Rackham. Read became a soldier, and fought in northern Europe. Then she sailed to the Caribbean, where she also met Rackham. He persuaded the women to join his company and their lives changed forever.

▼ *Anne Bonny and Mary Read disguised themselves as men.*

Anne Bonny

Born: 1698, in Ireland

Died: 1782, in South Carolina, North America

Occupation: Pirate

Rackham's arrest caused a sensation. When Captain Jonathan Barnet caught up with him, Rackham and most of his crew were too drunk to fight. Only two of the company fought back. When they were overpowered, they were found to be women dressed as men —Bonny and Read. The women were sentenced to hang, along with Rackham and his men. However, as both of them were pregnant, they were allowed to live.

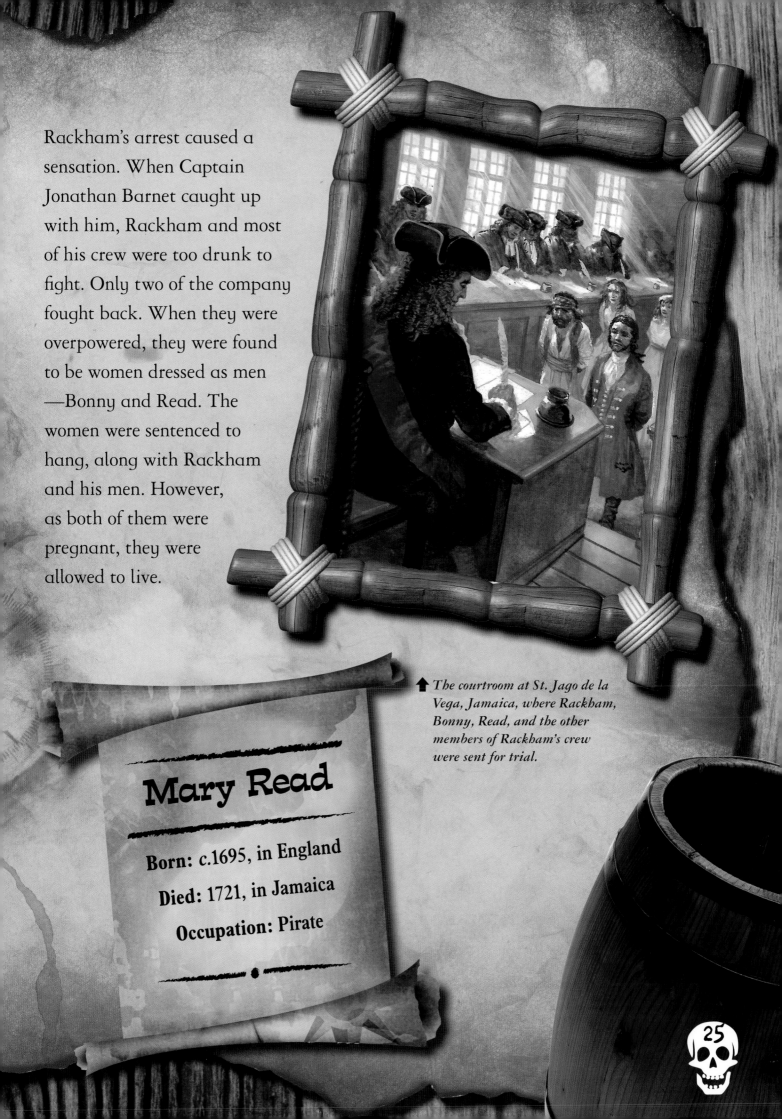

⬆ *The courtroom at St. Jago de la Vega, Jamaica, where Rackham, Bonny, Read, and the other members of Rackham's crew were sent for trial.*

Mary Read

Born: c.1695, in England

Died: 1721, in Jamaica

Occupation: Pirate

Punishments for prisoners and pirates

When pirates captured a ship or raided a town, they sometimes took prisoners.

Prisoners were usually held in return for goods or valuable information. Blackbeard once traded a group of prisoners for a chest of medicine—an odd trade for a pirate to make! If pirates thought that their prisoners knew where treasure was, they had ways of getting the information out of them, all of which involved cruelty.

➡ *The cat o' nine tails was a leather whip with several strands. Along the strands were sharp pieces of metal and pins.*

It was the quartermaster's job to make prisoners speak up, which many did before they were punished. The very thought of being **flogged** with the **cat o' nine tails** was often enough to loosen a prisoner's tongue.

⬅ *Towing was a punishment used to weaken a man. If he failed to keep his head above the water, he drowned.*

↑ *Marooning meant that a man was left alone on an island. He could wait for years before another ship came his way.*

The quartermaster carried out some of the worst punishments on pirates themselves. It was a way of keeping the company disciplined, letting the crew know what would happen if they disobeyed orders or broke the ship's articles. Pirates of the Caribbean never made a person "walk the plank"—a made-up punishment used in storybooks and films.

Pirate punishments

Blooding Pricked and spiked with knives and pins.

Ducking Splashed up and down in the sea.

Flogging Lashed with the cat o' nine tails.

Hanging Hanged by the neck until dead.

Keel-hauling Dragged under the ship, side to side.

Man overboard Thrown off the ship, and left to drown.

Marooning Abandoned on an island.

Moses' law Given 39 lashes with the cat.

One man island Left to drift with a plank of wood.

Towing Pulled along at the end of a rope behind the ship.

Pirate hunters: the end of pirates in the Caribbean

Pirates were masters of the Caribbean for only a few years and most had very short careers.

The end began when places such as New Providence stopped being safe havens for them. When Woodes Rogers became governor there, the first thing he did was offer a pardon to about 500 pirates.

SHIVER ME TIMBERS!

The bodies of some executed pirates, like John Rackham's, were wrapped in chains or iron cages and left to hang, where they slowly rotted away. It was a grizzly sight, and was meant to scare people off becoming pirates themselves.

Many accepted it, and in return for giving up piracy they were left alone. However, some pirates could not, or would not, change their "vile course of life," as Governor Rogers described piracy. These were the pirates who were tracked down by pirate hunters, sent out by governors to bring them to justice.

◀ *Despite having many cannon on their ships, pirates were outgunned by the pirate hunters who came after them.*

↑ *Bartholmew Roberts was killed by* grapeshot *fired from a navy warship (left). His men threw his body into the sea, rather than letting the naval officers hang it in chains.*

Pirates were rounded up and executed, often in groups. In 1718, Stede Bonnet was hanged with 30 others in Charleston, North Carolina. In 1722, 40 pirates were sent to the **gallows** in Kingston, Jamaica, and the following year, 26 men came to the same end in Newport, Rhode Island. By 1730, the pirates of the Caribbean had been defeated.

← *Stede Bonnet was hanged for piracy in 1718. He held onto a small bunch of flowers—a sign that he was sorry for all the wrong that he had done.*

29

GLOSSARY

Archeologist
A person who studies the remains of the past, on land and under water.

Articles
A set of rules that pirates were expected to follow.

Booty
Goods stolen by thieves. Also called loot or plunder.

Bow
The front of a ship.

Buccaneer
An outlaw who lived on the Caribbean islands and became a pirate.

Calico
A type of cotton.

Cannon
A large gun or guns on wheels that fired cannonballs and other types of shot.

Cat o' nine tails
A whip of nine knotted rope cords fastened to a handle. It was used against crew members and prisoners.

Chain shot
A type of shot fired from a cannon—two iron balls joined by a chain.

Company
The crew of a pirate ship.

Crew
The people who worked on a ship. Also called the company.

Doubloon
A Spanish gold coin used in Spain and the Caribbean.

Flagship
The main ship used by a pirate captain or navy commander.

Flintlock pistol
A type of pistol fired by a spark from a piece of flint.

Flog
To lash, or beat, with a whip or stick.

Fuse
A piece of material that a flame travels along to ignite, or set off, an explosion.

Gallows
A structure used for killing criminals by hanging them from a rope.

Governor
A person in charge of a place.

Grapeshot
A type of shot fired from a cannon— a mass of small iron balls.

Grappling hook
A four-pronged iron hook on a rope. It was used to pull one ship alongside another ship, so it could be boarded.

Haven
A safe place, or hideaway.

Jolly Roger
The nickname for any pirate flag.

Knight
To give someone the title of knight as a reward.

Loot
Goods stolen by thieves. Also called booty or plunder.

Maroon
To be abandoned on an island.

Mast
A tall pole that the sails of a ship hang on.

Merchant ship
A ship designed to transport goods.

Pardon
To forgive mistakes or offences, or to cancel a person's punishment.

Peace treaty
When opposite sides agree to be on friendly, peaceful terms.

Peso
A Spanish silver coin used in Spain and the Caribbean. Also called a piece of eight because it had the number eight on it, showing it was worth eight *reales*.

Piece of eight
The nickname for a Spanish peso or eight *reales* coin.

Plunder
To steal, or goods stolen by thieves. Also called loot or booty.

Privateer
A person who has permission from his government or ruler to attack and steal goods from their country's enemy.

Prize
A ship taken as a reward.

Quartermaster
The second-in-command on a ship, in charge of punishments.

Rigging
The ropes, posts, and chains that hold up a ship's sails.

Sloop
A fast, single-masted ship.

Tavern
A place where alcoholic drinks were consumed. Another word for an inn.

Vessel
A ship or large boat.

INDEX

Arot, Louis 5

Barnet, Jonathan 23, 25
Bellamy, Samuel 7, 16, 18–19
Blackbeard 4, 5, 6, 7, 8, 12–13, 15, 16,
    17, 26
Bonnet, Stede 15, 29
Bonny, Anne 7, 23, 24–25
buccaneers 6, 7, 10, 16

Calico Jack 22
cannon 4, 5, 8, 14, 20, 21, 28
cat o' nine tails 26, 27
Concorde 4, 5, 8

doubloons 21

gold 5, 18, 19, 21
Golden Age of piracy 6, 16

Hornigold, Benjamin 12

Jane 13
Jolly Roger 14, 15

Maynard, Robert 13
merchant ships 4, 8, 18, 20
Modyford, Thomas 10, 11
Morgan, Sir Henry 7, 10–11

navy 8, 13, 17, 29

pieces of eight 21
pirate hunters 28
pistols 21, 22
privateers 17

Queen Anne's Revenge 5, 12, 13

Rackham, John (Jack) 7, 15, 16, 22–23,
    24, 25, 28
Read, Mary 7, 23, 24–25
Roberts, Bartholomew 15, 29
Rogers, Woodes 17, 22, 23, 28

safe havens 16–17, 28
ship's articles 9, 14
silver 5, 11, 18, 21
slaves 4, 5, 18
sloops 4, 5, 8, 9, 12, 14, 17, 18, 20, 23
Sultana 18
swords 14, 20, 22

Teach, Edward *see Blackbeard*

warships 8, 17, 20, 29
Whydah 18–19
William 23